Dear Parent:

Congratulations! Your child is taking the first steps on an exciting journey. The destination? Independent reading!

STEP INTO READING® will help your child get there. The program offers books at five levels that accompany children from their first attempts at reading to reading success. Each step includes fun stories, fiction and nonfiction, and colorful art. There are also Step into Reading Sticker Books, Step into Reading Math Readers, Step into Reading Write-In Readers, Step into Reading Phonics Readers, and Step into Reading Phonics First Steps! Boxed Sets—a complete literacy program with something to interest every child.

Learning to Read, Step by Step!

Ready to Read Preschool–Kindergarten
• big type and easy words • rhyme and rhythm • picture clues
For children who know the alphabet and are eager to begin reading.

Reading with Help Preschool–Grade 1
• basic vocabulary • short sentences • simple stories
For children who recognize familiar words and sound out new words with help.

Reading on Your Own Grades 1–3
• engaging characters • easy-to-follow plots • popular topics
For children who are ready to read on their own.

Reading Paragraphs Grades 2–3
• challenging vocabulary • short paragraphs • exciting stories
For newly independent readers who read simple sentences with confidence.

Ready for Chapters Grades 2–4
• chapters • longer paragraphs • full-color art
For children who want to take the plunge into chapter books but still like colorful pictures.

STEP INTO READING® is designed to give every child a successful reading experience. The grade levels are only guides. Children can progress through the steps at their own speed, developing confidence in their reading, no matter what their grade.

Remember, a lifetime love of reading starts with a single step!

For my parents,
Roger and Patricia Fletcher Guess,
who nurtured creativity
—J.G.M.

For my sister, who has always loved horses
—T.W.

Acknowledgments: With special thanks to Jennifer Stermer,
Curator of Collections of the International Museum of the
Horse at the Kentucky Horse Park in Lexington, Kentucky, for
her time and expertise in reviewing this book.

Photo courtesy of the Kentucky Horse Park.
Text copyright © 2005 by Jennifer Guess McKerley. Illustrations copyright © 2005 by Terry
Widener. All rights reserved under International and Pan-American Copyright Conventions.
Published in the United States by Random House Children's Books, a division of Random
House, Inc., New York, and simultaneously in Canada by Random House of Canada Limited,
Toronto.

www.stepintoreading.com

Educators and librarians, for a variety of teaching tools, visit us at
www.randomhouse.com/teachers

Library of Congress Cataloging-in-Publication Data
McKerley, Jennifer Guess.
Man o' War : best racehorse ever / by Jennifer Guess McKerley ; illustrated by Terry Widener.
  p. cm. — (Step into reading. Step 3)
ISBN 0-375-83164-9 (trade) — ISBN 0-375-93164-3 (lib. bdg.)
1. Man o' War (Race horse)—Juvenile literature. 2. Race horses—United States—Biography—
Juvenile literature. I. Widener, Terry, ill. II. Title. III. Series.
SF355.M3M36 2005   798.4'0092'9—dc22   2004016816

Printed in the United States of America   First Edition   10 9 8 7 6 5 4 3 2 1

STEP INTO READING, RANDOM HOUSE, and the Random House colophon are registered trademarks
of Random House, Inc.

STEP INTO READING®
STEP 3

MAN O' WAR
Best Racehorse Ever

by Jennifer Guess McKerley
illustrated by Terry Widener

Random House 🏠 New York

Man o' War was
a great racehorse.
Some say he was
the greatest ever!

He was born in 1917.
But he did not look
like a racehorse then!

When Man o' War

was one year old,

a horse trainer named

Louis Feustel came to see him.

Louis's boss, Samuel Riddle,

wanted to buy a new racehorse.

"This colt wobbles," Louis fussed.

But the colt seemed strong.

And his eyes looked full of spirit.

"I'll take him," Louis said.

Louis took Man o' War
to the Riddle farm in Maryland.
"We will make a champion
out of you," he promised.
The colt ate like a horse
and grew

and grew.

Man o' War did not like

to wear a saddle.

So he played tricks.

When the stable boys saddled him,

he puffed out his chest

before they pulled the belt tight.

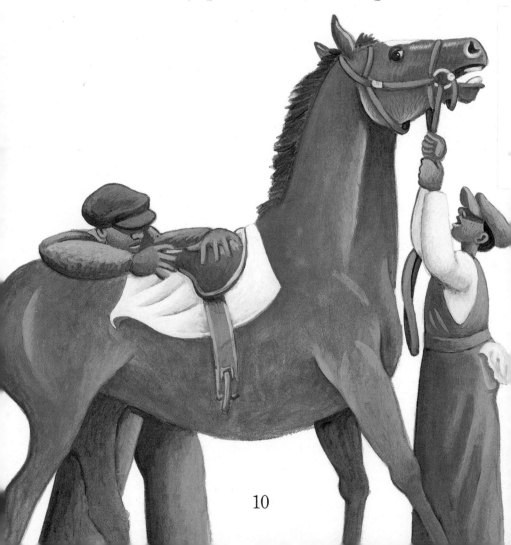

Then he let his breath out.

That made the belt hang loose.

He puffed—they pulled.

Finally, they would get

the saddle on right!

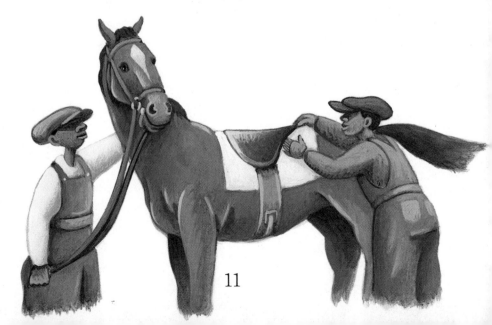

But Man o' War
was never mean—
just lively.
The stable boys liked
this friendly horse.
They called him "Big Red"
because his brown coat
shone red in the sun.

Man o' War loved to run.

And he liked to fidget!

He would not slow down

long enough to be trained.

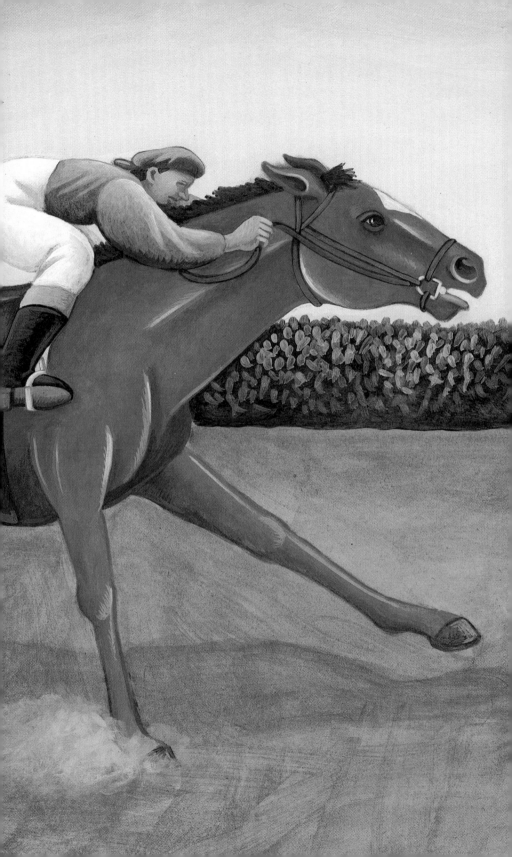

Louis had an idea.

Maybe an older horse

would calm Man o' War down.

Louis brought in a horse

named Major Treat.

The two horses

became buddies!

They liked to stay side by side.

Now Man o' War was

happy to train.

When Man o' War
turned two years old,
he didn't wobble anymore.
He was graceful and fast!
"He's ready to race," said Louis.

Louis took Man o' War
to New York for his first race.
When the flag dropped,
Man o' War galloped
past the other horses.
He won by six lengths!

Man o' War won
five more races in a row.
But Louis was worried.
The owner of Golden Broom
wanted a private match.
Golden Broom had beaten
Man o' War during practice.
"Can Man o' War win this time?"
Mr. Riddle asked Louis.
There was only one way
to find out!

Man o' War charged ahead.

He dashed across the finish line—

first!

"We have a champion!"

shouted Louis.

The crowds agreed.

They loved Man o' War.

He was powerful and fast.

But he still liked to fidget.

He even danced about

at the starting line.

The playful champion

won their hearts.

He'd won every race he ran.

Then came the race

no one would forget.

As usual,

Man o' War danced in circles

to the starting line.

But this time,

the jockey who rode Man o' War

didn't turn him around

fast enough.

When the race began,

Man o' War faced the wrong way!

Finally, Man o' War
got turned around.

He thundered down the track.

He passed all the horses but one.

A horse named Upset won,

but only by half a length.

Ten days later,
Man o' War raced again.
He beat all nine horses—
including Upset.
Soon he was named
Horse of the Year!

At the age of three,

Man o' War was a

grand racehorse.

His long legs took huge leaps.

He stood over sixteen hands high.

Still, Mr. Riddle didn't want
to work Man o' War too hard.
So he didn't enter him
in the Kentucky Derby.

The Derby,

the Preakness,

and the Belmont Stakes

were the top races.

A horse that won all three

became a Triple Crown winner.

Man o' War won

the Preakness and the Belmont!

He even set a world record

for speed.

Fans crowded around his stall.

Sportswriters wrote about him.

He was the most famous

horse in the world.

But now owners refused

to race their horses against him.

What was the use?

Their horses didn't have a chance.

Then Upset's trainer said,

"I've got another horse

that can beat Man o' War."

It was John P. Grier.

Man o' War had lost only one race.

Would this be the second?

Across America,
families gathered around
their radios to listen to the race.

"John P. Grier leads!"

the announcer called.

"Wait! It's Man o' War!

He wins again!"

Then Man o' War raced Sir Barton.
Sir Barton was a
Triple Crown winner.
"Man o' War hasn't won
a Triple Crown,"
fans worried.

The two horses took off.

Man o' War dashed far ahead.

"Man o' War beats

the Triple Crown winner!"

cried the announcer.

After Man o' War turned four,

Mr. Riddle decided

not to race him anymore.

He had beaten the fifty best

racehorses in America.

He'd set eight records for speed.

Mr. Riddle was offered

one million dollars!

But he refused to sell his champ.

Man o' War went to live
on Faraway Farm in Kentucky.
His friend Major Treat went, too.
Artists came to paint his picture.
And two million fans visited him.

His greatest fan was Will Harbut.
Will took care of Man o' War.
He told visitors about all
the old racehorses there.
But he saved his
favorite horse for last.

"Here's Man o' War himself,"
he'd say.
"He broke all the records.
He beat all the other horses.
He's the best racehorse ever."

MAJOR TREAT

MAN O' WAR

Each year Mr. Riddle gave
Man o' War a birthday party.
Fans sent cakes made of oats.
Man o' War even ate the candles—
because they were carrots!
When Man o' War
turned twenty-one,
fans turned on the radio
and heard the party.

In 1947, Man o' War died.
He was thirty years old.
Thousands of fans
went to his funeral.
Many more listened
to it on the radio.

Ten years later,

Man o' War was chosen for

the Racing Hall of Fame.

In 1999, he was named

the Greatest Horse

of the Century.

Author's Note

Man o' War had sixty-four
sons and grandsons
who became racing champions.
He was Seabiscuit's grandfather.
Man o' War is buried at
the Kentucky Horse Park
in Lexington.
His statue stands at the entrance.